RAINBOWS

David Whitfield

www.av2books.com

AV² provides enriched content that supplements and complements this book. Weigl's AV² books strive to create inspired learning and engage young minds in a total learning experience.

Your AV² Media Enhanced books come alive with...

Audio
Listen to sections of the book read aloud.

Key Words
Study vocabulary, and complete a matching word activity.

Video
Watch informative video clips.

Quizzes
Test your knowledge.

Embedded Weblinks
Gain additional information for research.

Slide Show
View images and captions, and prepare a presentation.

Try This!
Complete activities and hands-on experiments.

... and much, much more!

Go to www.av2books.com, and enter this book's unique code.

BOOK CODE

T758468

AV² by Weigl brings you media enhanced books that support active learning.

Published by AV² by Weigl
350 5th Avenue, 59th Floor
New York, NY 10118
Website: www.av2books.com   www.weigl.com

Library of Congress Control Number: 2012941988
ISBN 978-1-61913-099-9 (hard cover)
ISBN 978-1-61913-546-8 (soft cover)

Printed in the United States of America in North Mankato, Minnesota
1 2 3 4 5 6 7 8 9 16 15 14 13 12

062012
WEP170512

Editor Aaron Carr
Design Ken Clarke

Every reasonable effort has been made to trace ownership and to obtain permission to reprint copyright material. The publishers would be pleased to have any errors or omissions brought to their attention so that they may be corrected in subsequent printings.

Weigl acknowledges Getty Images as its primary image supplier for this title.

CONTENTS

AV² Book Code 2

Studying Rainbows 5

Colors of the Rainbow 6

Rainbow Variations .8

How Rainbows Form 10

Sky Technology 12

Double Rainbows 14

Lunar Rainbows 16

Rainbow Proverbs .18

What is a Mathematician? 19

Seven Facts About Rainbows 20

Rainbow Brain Teasers 21

Science in Action .22

Key Words/Index .23

Log on to www.av2books.com 24

Human activity is changing the world. Gases that humans have put into the atmosphere trap heat from the Sun. This causes more water to **evaporate** and fall back to Earth as **precipitation**. This process causes storms to occur more often and to be more severe. As a side effect of this process, there may be more rainbows seen around the world today than at any time in the past hundred years.

Studying Rainbows

Nature creates rainbows in the sky. Rainbows can be found almost anywhere in the world where there is rain and sunshine. They may appear after a rainstorm, when the Sun is shining.

Although there is no record of when the first rainbow was seen, humans have been interested in rainbows since ancient times. Ancient peoples thought rainbows appeared magically in the sky. They created **proverbs**, songs, and legends about them.

■ Ancient peoples often used rainbows in art to symbolize a bridge between Earth and the heavens above.

Colors of the Rainbow

White light is made of many different colors. These colors are often seen in the sky during or after rainfall. Rainbow colors are created when sunlight shines on raindrops in the sky. Sunlight is made up of many colors of light people can see. It also contains colors people cannot see. When all colors are mixed together, sunlight looks white. However, when sunlight is refracted, or bent, in a raindrop, it separates into seven colors. These are the colors in a rainbow.

■ Billions of raindrops are needed to make a rainbow.

BENDING LIGHT

Sunlight follows a straight line when it moves through the air. If it enters another substance, such as water or glass, it changes direction or bends. This bending is called refraction.

Light refraction can be studied using a prism. A prism is a triangle-shaped piece of glass or **acrylic**. When sunlight strikes the prism, the light does not shine through in a straight line. The light slows down and is bent as it enters the prism. Some colors of light bend more than others. Violet bends the most, and red bends the least.

The bending separates the light into seven colors: red, orange, yellow, green, blue, indigo, and violet. When a single rainbow is seen, red is at the top and violet is at the bottom.

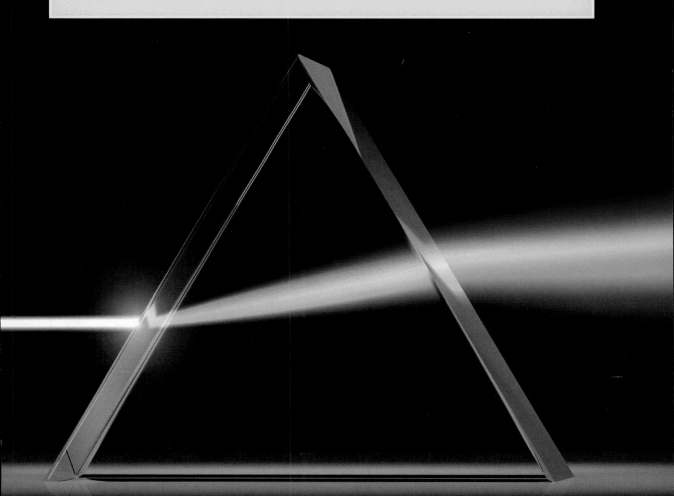

Rainbow Variations

White light can be scattered into its colors in many different ways. Though rainbows are most often seen in the sky, the process that creates them is very common. Ice crystals, sprays of water, and even some other liquids can produce rainbows under the right conditions.

◼ Sundogs are most visible when the Sun is low on the horizon.

SUNDOGS AND HALOS

On some cold, clear days in winter, rainbow-like colors can be seen. When the Sun shines on ice crystals, a bright halo may appear around the Sun. Bright spots on either side of the halo are called sundogs. Most sundogs are white, but sometimes they are red on the inside and blue on the outside.

LOW RAINBOWS

Rain is not necessary for rainbows to appear. However, there must be moisture in the air. Rainbows can be seen near waterfalls, as the Sun shines on the mist. Rainbows can also be seen in sprays made by garden hoses, lawn sprinklers, and fountains. Sometimes, rainbows can be seen in spray from a boat.

SOAP AND OIL

Rainbow colors can be seen in soap bubbles or in oil spills on a wet road. They are not true rainbows, but can show the same colors. Unlike rainbows, colors in bubbles and oil spills can shift and change. They swirl with the movement of the liquid they are in. When people look at this type of rainbow, the colors may change, depending on the point of view.

How Rainbows Form

Rainbows form when rain falls in one part of the sky while the Sun shines in another. Sunlight shining on raindrops in the sky creates a rainbow.

When sunlight strikes a raindrop, the raindrop acts like a prism. Each color of light refracts at a different angle. The light separates as it passes through the raindrop. After the light is bent inside the raindrop, it is reflected, or bounced, back toward the source of light. Then, the light bends once more when it exits the raindrop.

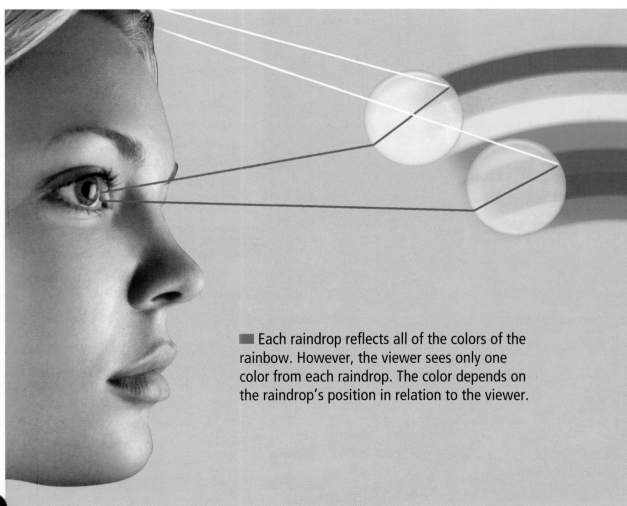

■ Each raindrop reflects all of the colors of the rainbow. However, the viewer sees only one color from each raindrop. The color depends on the raindrop's position in relation to the viewer.

REFLECTED LIGHT

People seldom notice that the Sun is always behind them when they see a rainbow. The center of a rainbow **arc** always appears in the sky opposite the Sun. This is because the raindrop reflects the sunlight back toward the Sun. In order for someone to see the rainbow, the Sun must be behind the viewer. The viewer's eyes see the colors as they reflect back from the raindrops.

Sky Technology

Geographic Information System

Special computers called Geographic Information Systems (GIS) gather information about Earth. Scientists use GIS to map **air pollution** in cities and towns. Results are posted on the Internet so people can read about the types and amount of pollution where they live.

Telescopes

Telescopes help people see objects that are far away. **Astronomers** use them to observe space objects, such as stars, planets, and whole **galaxies**. Telescopes make distant objects appear closer by collecting light. Telescopes can collect more light than the human eye.

Weather Satellite

Weather satellites are spacecraft that circle Earth. They provide a weather watch on the entire planet. Weather satellites take pictures of Earth's atmosphere. These pictures help meteorologists predict storms and other weather patterns. These satellites also carry special instruments that record information on computers. They monitor events in the atmosphere, such as auroras, dust storms, pollution, and cloud systems.

Radar

Meteorologists gather huge amounts of information in order to predict the weather. **Radar** can tell people what is inside a cloud. This can be rain or hail. Radar can also track a storm that is coming. It helps meteorologists warn people if the storm is dangerous.

Double Rainbows

Sometimes, two rainbows form together. The rainbows are seen one above the other. When there are two rainbows, the lower one is called the primary rainbow. The higher one is the secondary rainbow.

Sunlight must be very strong to create two rainbows. The sunlight is reflected once in raindrops to make the primary rainbow. Then, if the light is reflected again, it creates a secondary rainbow. This rainbow is not as bright as the primary rainbow.

■ A primary rainbow is violet on the bottom and red on top. In secondary rainbows, the colors are reversed. Violet is at the top, and red is at the bottom.

Bright Sky

The sky inside or below a rainbow is often brighter than the sky above or outside the rainbow. This is because light that is not reflected into the colors of the rainbow is scattered below it. Since this is white light, the sky looks brighter.

When there is a double rainbow in the sky, there is often a dark band between the two rainbows. This dark area is called Alexander's Dark Band. It is named after Alexander of Aphrodisias, a Greek **philosopher**. He first described it hundreds of years ago. This area is darker than the rest of the sky because the light reflected from the raindrops in this area is scattered above or below. This light does not reach an observer's eyes.

■ Alexander of Aphrodisias first observed the dark band between a double rainbow in AD 200.

Lunar Rainbows

Sometimes, the moon can create a rainbow at night. This kind of rainbow is called a **lunar** rainbow. Lunar rainbows are rare.

Lunar rainbows are not as bright as rainbows that appear during the day. In fact, lunar rainbows are sometimes so pale that they appear as a gray, white, or silver arc in the night sky. Like daytime rainbows, the source of light for lunar rainbows is sunlight. However, at night the sunlight bounces off the surface of the moon and reflects to Earth.

■ Reflected light from the Moon causes lunar rainbows to appear paler than regular rainbows.

As the Sun sets, the sky often turns red. This is because the atmosphere refracts the Sun's light, much like a giant water droplet. The sky turns red because the blue and green parts of the light have been scattered away. Rainbows that occur at this time of day can often appear to be a single color. These single-color rainbows are known as monochrome rainbows, and are most often red. Moonbows contain all the colors of a normal rainbow, but they are so faint that they often appear to be a monochrome white.

Rainbow Folklore

Rainbows have captured the imaginations of people around the world. They are featured in the folklore of many cultures. In some African **myths**, the rainbow was a giant snake that hunted when the sun went down. Some European tales say that a person who travels under a rainbow will be transformed into a different gender.

IRELAND

One of the most popular rainbow stories is from Ireland. In Irish folklore, tricky and sometimes mean-spirited creatures known as **leprechauns** are said to bury pots of gold at the ends of rainbows.

EASTERN EUROPE

Some stories from Eastern Europe also feature the rainbow as a giant snake. The snake drank water from seas, lakes, and rivers. The snake then sprinkled the water over the land as rain.

FINLAND

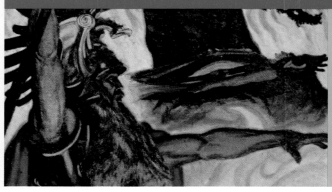

Long ago, people in Finland believed a rainbow was the bow used by the Thunder God to shoot arrows made of lightning.

Rainbow Proverbs

For **centuries**, people have tried to **forecast** the weather. Long before weather reports on the internet, television, or radio, people looked for weather clues in nature. They used proverbs to explain the weather. Some proverbs were based on the science of nature. This is an example of a weather proverb:

Rainbow to windward, foul fall the day,
Rainbow to leeward, rain runs away.

This proverb is based on the fact that if the wind is blowing from the direction of a rainbow, rain is coming toward the observer. If the wind is blowing toward a rainbow, then rain is moving away from the observer.

 A common proverb says, "after the storm comes the rainbow."

What is a Mathematician?

Mathematicians are scientists who study numbers and quantities. Some only study mathematics, while others apply this study to other fields, such as engineering and physics.

René Descartes combined his knowledge of angles, space, and distance with his knowledge of how light behaved. This knowledge allowed him to discover how rainbows are formed. Today, mathematicians unlock the basic principles necessary to make valuable technology function. Their work also provides tools to improve the study of other fields of science, such as biology and physics.

René Descartes

René Descartes was a French philosopher and mathematician. In 1637, he published his research. He said light was refracted in a raindrop then reflected back out. To learn about how water affected light, Descartes made a model of a single water droplet using a glass ball full of water.

■ Mathematicians work in a wide range of fields, including science, computer science, teaching, research, and finance.

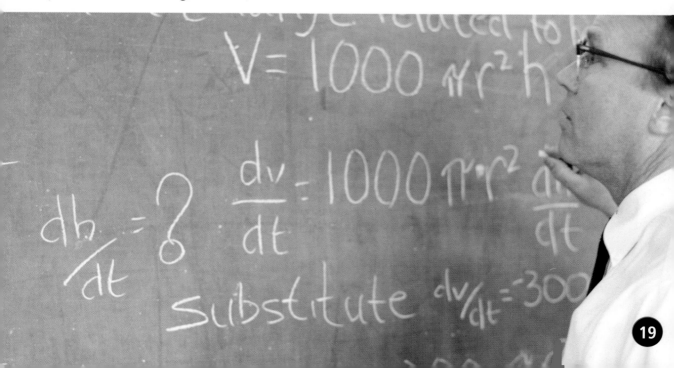

Seven Facts About Rainbows

When viewed from an airplane with the Sun behind it, a rainbow looks like a complete circle.

Large raindrops produce brighter red, orange, yellow, and green colors in the rainbow. Small raindrops produce brighter violets.

It is impossible to reach the "end" of a rainbow. Moving only changes the angles of light that reach an observer's eye.

Rainbows are rarely seen at noon, when the Sun is high in the sky.

Rainbows appear to have seven main colors, but are actually made up of every color of visible light.

Scientists believe that Titan, one of Saturn's moons, might have rainbows. Titan's air contains a gas that could create rainbows when the Sun shines.

Ancient Norse people believed that a rainbow bridge called Bifrost connected the worlds of humans and the gods.

Rainbow Brain Teasers

1 What acts like a prism in the sky, bending light to create a rainbow?

2 In which season do sundogs appear?

3 What kind of light is needed to see a rainbow in the sky?

4 Who discovered that light was refracted in a raindrop and then reflected back out?

5 Which seven colors are seen in a rainbow?

6 Where must the Sun be for a person to see a rainbow?

7 How is a secondary rainbow different from a primary rainbow?

8 What is the rarest type of rainbow?

9 Do large or small raindrops produce brighter yellows, oranges, and reds in a rainbow?

10 Besides raindrops, what can create rainbows?

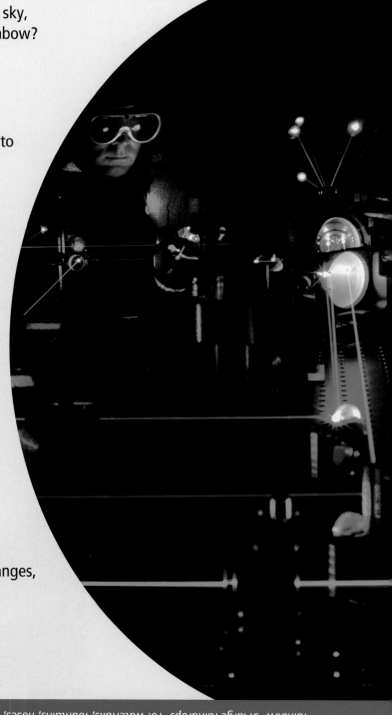

Science in Action

Make Your Own Rainbow
This activity should be done with an adult.

garden hose

watering nozzle

sunlight

partner

Directions

1 Have your partner attach the nozzle to the end of the hose, and set it to a fine spray.

2 With your back to the sun, have your partner spray a mist of water into the air.

3 Adjust your position until you can see a rainbow. Are all of the colors present? Can you see the second rainbow?

4 Change positions with your partner. Did he or she see the same things you did?

Key Words

acrylic: a type of plastic

air pollution: harmful materials, such as chemicals and gas, that make air dirty

arc: a curve or part of a circle

centuries: hundreds of years

evaporate: to turn from a liquid into a gas, or vapor

forecast: predict

galaxies: large groups of stars

leprechauns: magical creatures in Irish folklore who must give his hidden treasure to whoever catches him

lunar: relating to the moon

mathematician: a person who studies mathematics

myths: legends or stories passed on for many generations

philosopher: a person who studies the nature of reality

precipitation: water released from clouds as rain, snow, or hail

proverb: well-known expression that states a general truth or gives advice

radar: a system that uses radio waves to locate objects in the atmosphere

Index

Alexander's Dark Band 15
angle 10, 19, 20
arc 11, 16

Descartes, René 19, 21
double rainbow 14, 15

lunar rainbows 16, 21

mathematician 19
moonbows 16
myths 17

primary rainbow 14, 21
prism 7, 10, 21
proverbs 5, 18

reflected 10, 11, 14, 15, 16, 19, 21
refracted 6, 7, 10, 16, 19, 21

secondary rainbow 14, 21
sundogs 8, 9, 21
sunlight 6, 7, 10, 11, 14, 16, 21, 22

Titan 20

waterfall 9, 21
weather 13, 18

Log on to www.av2books.com

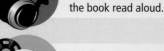

AV² by Weigl brings you media enhanced books that support active learning. Go to www.av2books.com, and enter the special code found on page 2 of this book. You will gain access to enriched and enhanced content that supplements and complements this book. Content includes video, audio, weblinks, quizzes, a slide show, and activities.

Audio
Listen to sections of the book read aloud.

Video
Watch informative video clips.

Embedded Weblinks
Gain additional information for research.

Try This!
Complete activities and hands-on experiments.

WHAT'S ONLINE?

Try This!	**Embedded Weblinks**	**Video**	**EXTRA FEATURES**
Complete a rainbow activity.	Learn more about rainbows.	Watch a video about rainbows.	**Audio** Listen to sections of the book read aloud.
Identify the types of rainbows.	Find out more about how rainbows form.	Watch a video about the visible light spectrum.	
Try a light spectrum activity.	Read more about the visible light spectrum.		**Key Words** Study vocabulary, and complete a matching word activity.
Test your knowledge of rainbows.	Learn more about different types of rainbows.		
			Slide Show View images and captions, and prepare a presentation
			Quizzes Test your knowledge.

AV² was built to bridge the gap between print and digital. We encourage you to tell us what you like and what you want to see in the future.

Sign up to be an AV² Ambassador at www.av2books.com/ambassador.